Blood Su...

Written by Victoria Travers

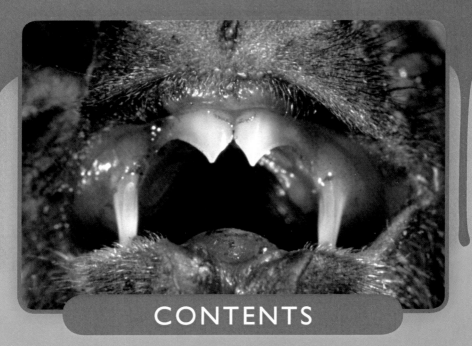

CONTENTS

Blood Suckers

Some animals eat blood to survive. The blood gives these animals all the food they need to live and grow. Blood is a liquid food and the best way to eat a liquid food is to suck it. Most blood-sucking animals take only a small amount of blood from their host.

vampire bats

Glossary:

host: the name given to an animal that a blood-sucking animal feeds off.

To get their food, blood-sucking animals need to find a host, attach themselves to the host and suck its blood.

These animals all suck blood to survive:

- mosquitoes
- ticks
- fleas
- lampreys
- leeches
- vampire bats.

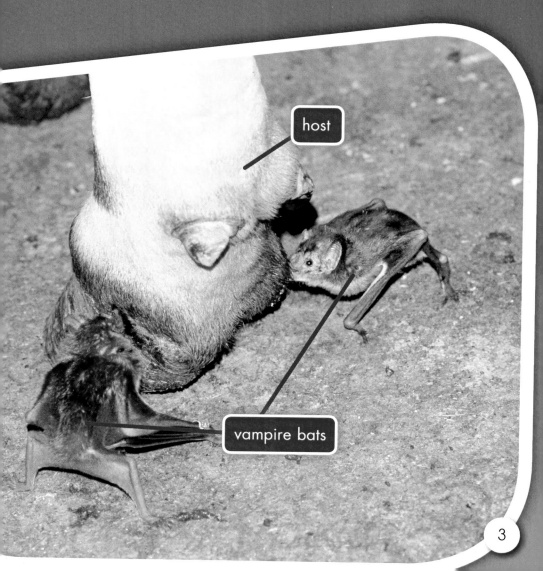

host

vampire bats

How Mosquitoes Suck Blood

Mosquitoes are insects. Only the female mosquitoes need to suck blood for food. Mosquitoes feed from mammals and birds.

Mosquitoes find their host by smelling the air that mammals and birds breathe out. When mosquitoes get close enough, they can also feel the heat of their host.

Mosquitoes suck the blood of mammals and birds by using their long, pointed proboscis.

Up close, the proboscis is jagged on the edges so that once it pokes through the skin it will not come out easily. The proboscis is hollow like a straw and the mosquito is able to suck blood up through it. Once a mosquito has eaten enough blood, it will take out its proboscis and fly away.

Glossary:

proboscis: part of a mosquito's mouth. It is sharp at the end for poking through skin.

mammals: warm-blooded animals such as humans, cows, dogs and horses

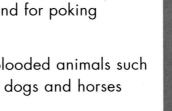

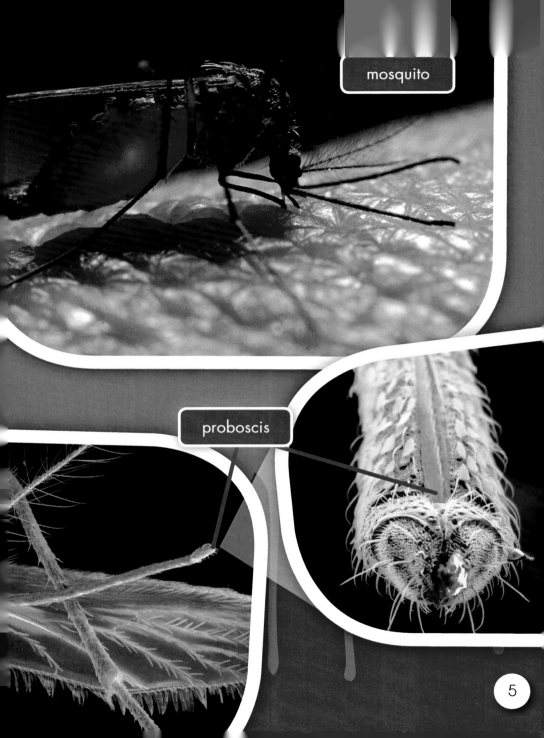

mosquito

proboscis

5

How Fleas Suck Blood

Fleas are tiny insects that feed off the blood of mammals and birds. They have no wings but can jump over 200 times their body size. This helps them to jump on to hosts as they pass by.

Fleas find their hosts by feeling movement in the air and the heat that the hosts make. Fleas are narrow and flat. This helps them to move easily between the hairs and feathers growing from a host's skin. Their mouth parts fit together to form a point. They use this point to puncture the skin and suck the blood.

mouth parts

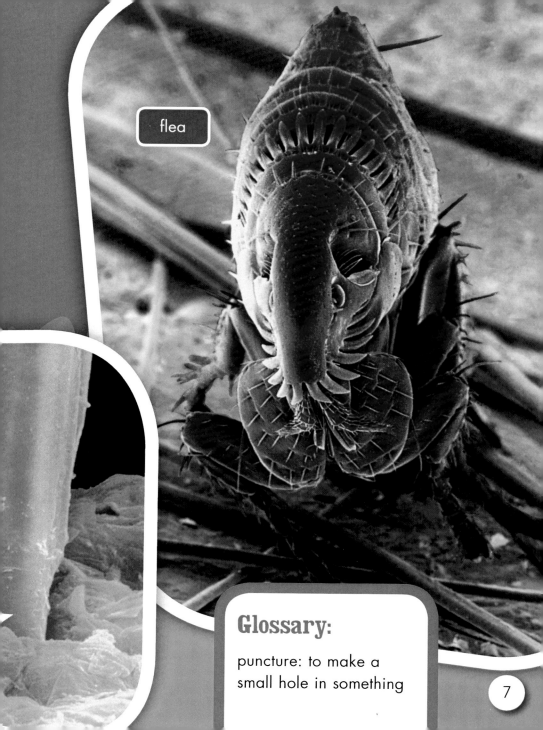

flea

Glossary:

puncture: to make a
small hole in something

How Leeches Suck Blood

Leeches are types of worms that live in damp or wet places, such as caves, rivers, streams or under piles of leaves. Leeches will feed from frogs, birds, fish and mammals. Leeches find their hosts by feeling the movement of the water or the air around where they live. Leeches creep towards a host until they touch it with their mouth.

Once the leech touches its host, it will puncture the skin with its tiny teeth. It then uses a special slime to glue itself to the host while it sucks blood. Once the leech is full of blood it falls off and crawls somewhere dark to digest its liquid food. Leeches can live for many months between meals.

mouth of a leech

How a Leech Finds Its Host

The leech senses the vibrations from the movement of the host.

The leech attaches itself to the leg.

How Ticks Suck Blood

Ticks are members of the spider family. They feed on the blood of mammals and birds. When ticks are ready to feed, they crawl up blades of grass and wait for a host to pass by. They can feel the movement and heat of the host as well as smell the air it breathes out.

Once the tick has crawled on to the host, it uses its spear-like mouth to puncture the skin. It uses slime to glue itself to the host's skin so that it is hard to remove. The tick feeds on the blood and will fall off when it is full.

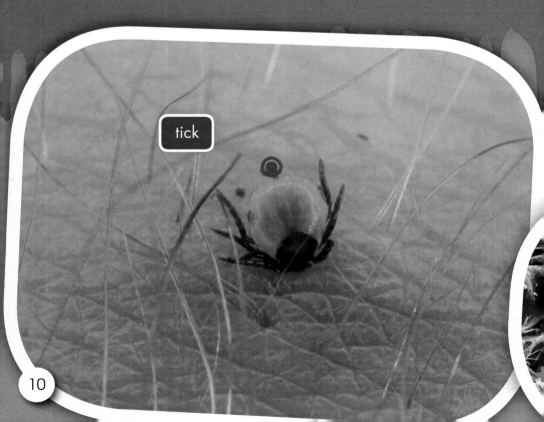

tick

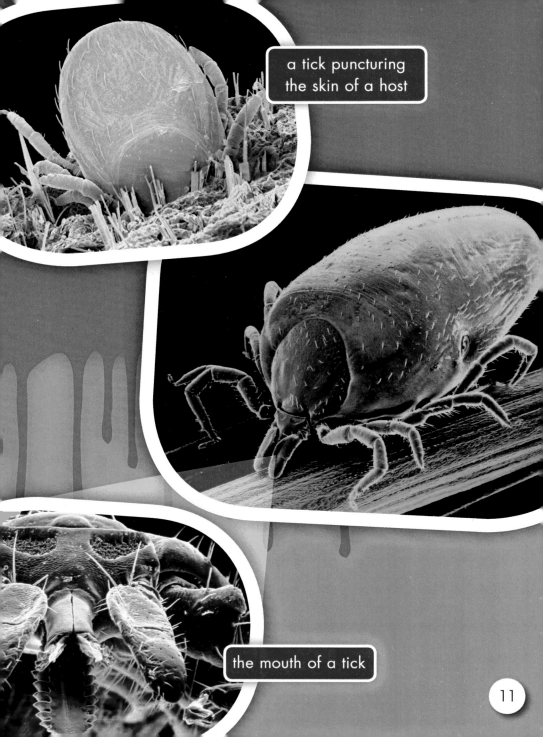

a tick puncturing
the skin of a host

the mouth of a tick

How Lampreys Suck Blood

A lamprey is a type of fish. It lives off the blood of other fish. Lampreys find their hosts mostly by sight. When the lamprey sees a host, it swims to it and sucks on to the skin of the fish with its mouth.

Lampreys use their tongue and teeth to scrape away the scales and skin of the fish so they can suck it's blood. Once the lamprey has grown large enough to lay eggs, it lets go of its host and swims away.

a lamprey attached to a fish

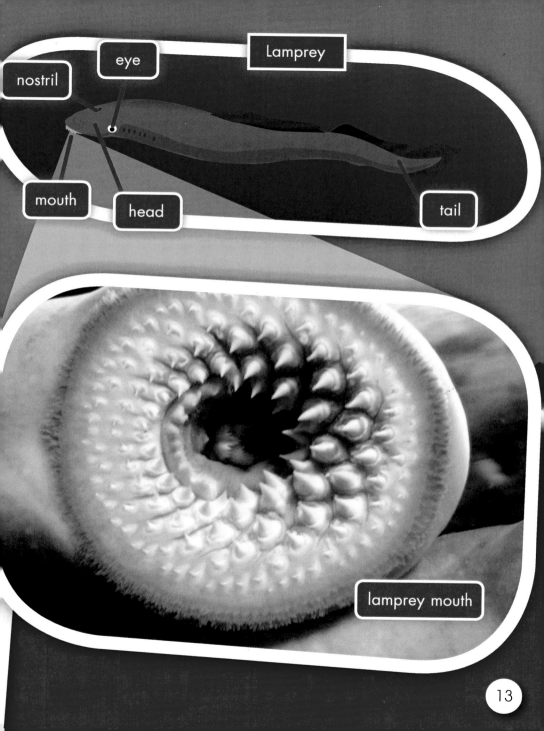

Lamprey

nostril

eye

mouth

head

tail

lamprey mouth

13

How Vampire Bats Suck Blood

Vampire bats are small, flying mammals that feed on blood. They are most active at night and sleep during the day. Vampire bats feed mostly on the blood of larger mammals such as cows.

Vampire bats have very good hearing. They can hear the slow breathing of a sleeping animal. When a vampire bat hears a sleeping host it will land close by and crawl over to it. Using its sharp teeth, it cuts away the host's hair and makes a deep cut in the skin. when the host starts bleeding, the vampire bat licks up the blood with its tongue. When it is full, the vampire bat flies away.

a vampire bat licking blood from a cow

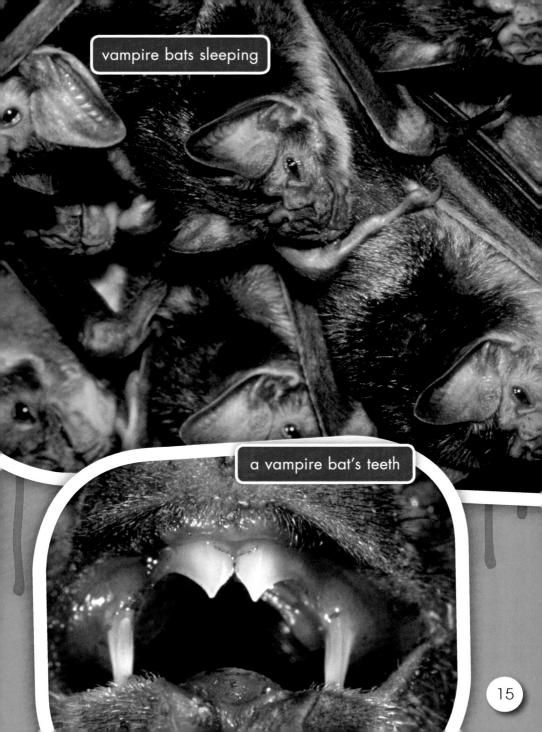

vampire bats sleeping

a vampire bat's teeth

Summary Table

Name of Blood Sucker	Type of Animal	Type of Host	How It Finds Its Host
mosquito	insect	mammals birds	smell smell heat
flea	insect	mammals birds	movement heat
leech	worm	fish mammals birds frogs	movement
tick	spider	mammals birds	movement heat smell
lamprey	fish	fish	sight
vampire bat	mammal	mammals	sound

Index

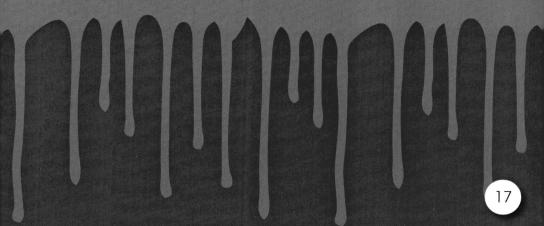

Explanations

Blood Suckers is an **explanation**.

An explanation explains **how** or **why** things happen.

An explanation has a topic:

Blood Suckers

An explanation has headings:

How Mosquitoes Suck Blood

How Fleas Suck Blood

How Leeches Suck Blood

How Ticks Suck Blood

Some information is put under headings:

How Vampire Bats Suck Blood

- crawls over to the host
- makes a deep cut with its teeth
- licks the blood with its tongue

Information can be shown in other ways.
This explanation has . . .

Labels   Bullet Points   Sequence Diagram

Captions   Photographs   Glossary

Illustrations

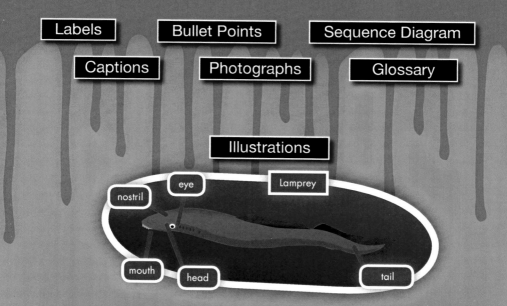

nostril   eye   Lamprey

mouth   head   tail

Guide Notes

Title: **Blood Suckers**

Stage: Fluency

Text Form: Informational Explanation

Approach: Guided Reading

Processes: Thinking Critically, Exploring Language, Processing Information

Written and Visual Focus: Contents Page, Bullet Points, Captions, Labels, Sequence Diagram, Illustrations, Index

THINKING CRITICALLY
(sample questions)
Before Reading – Establishing Prior Knowledge
•   What do you know about blood suckers?
Visualising the Text Content
•   What might you expect to see in this book?
•   What form of writing do you think will be used by the author?
Look at the contents page and index. Encourage the students to think about the information and make predictions about the text content.

After Reading – Interpretation
•   Why do you think that blood suckers take only a small amount of blood from each host?
•   Why do you think that only female mosquitoes suck blood?
•   Do you think the lamprey would hurt its host? Why or why not?
•   What things do mosquitoes, fleas and ticks have in common?
•   Do you think that vampire bats are good hunters? Why or why not?
•   Do you think that some blood suckers could serve a good purpose? Why or why not?
•   What do you know about blood suckers that you didn't know before?
•   What in the book helped you to understand the information?
•   What questions do you have after reading the text?

EXPLORING LANGUAGE

Terminology
Photograph credits, index, contents page, imprint information, ISBN number